# Animals Everywhere

Written by Tim Wilde

# Animals live

# in many places.

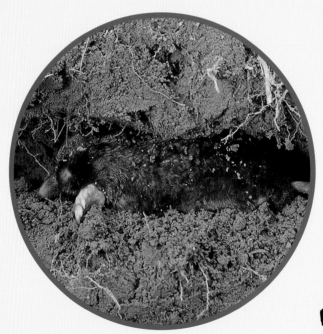

2

Some animals live
in the deep, blue sea.

dolphin

octopus

turtle

Some animals live

in green, leafy jungles.

gorilla

frog

tiger

Some animals live
in hot, dry deserts.

camels

scorpion

snake

9

Some animals live where

there is ice and snow.

polar bears

seal

penguins

11

Some animals live

under the ground.

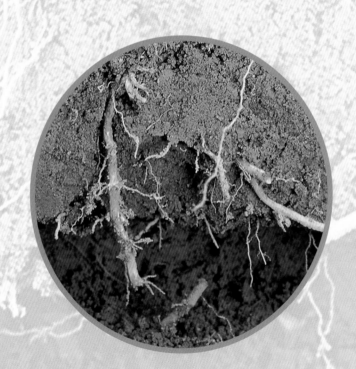

ants

mole

badgers

These animals are pets.

Where do they live?

# Index